THE LIFE OF A Rose

A BLUE PRINT FOR Prosperity

AVA COOPER

Table of Contents

Dedication

I would like to dedicate this book to my late grandfather, Taylor Cooper, and my grandmother, Ethel Cooper, my birth parents, all my beautiful boys. I would also like to dedicate this to my adoptive mother and father, as well as all my family members who have shown me love, guidance, compassion, concern, advice, and the direction that has helped shape the woman I am today. My time spent in Los Angeles and Hollywood has motivated me to strive for my full potential in life and to be a good woman and more importantly, a mother. I also want to acknowledge all my true mentors and spiritual leaders who have helped me understand that whatever I achieve in life is only by God's grace.

Chapter 1 –

My Mother and San Bernardino

It was a mundane Monday in San Bernardino, people were commuting to their morning shifts, and those that worked during the night were returning home from their night shifts. The indiscriminating fact about life in San Bernardino was everyone was going somewhere, but no one was actually settled. Everyone had different levels of aspirations; some were more ambitious than others, but each person living in the vicinity of San Bernardino was adamant about making their lifestyle better.

The era I want this book to start with is the 1970s. In these pages, I aim to recount the compelling story of Willow, a compassionate woman who confronted hardship throughout her formative years. Through her narrative, my aspiration is to ignite inspiration within you, encouraging you to strive for remarkable achievements in your own life. If just one reader of this book can go on to make a positive impact on the world, then I consider my mission a triumph. To embark on Willow's inspirational journey, let me transport you to the very place of her birth.

The city of San Bernardino, California, in the year 1974, was tremendously vibrant. It was located in the inland region of Southern California. People greeted each other respectfully and celebrated the commonness of their lifestyle. You see, you could be employed in an entirely different sector than your neighbor or your close friend, and your talents and skills could be profoundly different from your life partner or elder sibling, but you would still follow the same daily routine. An average day in the story of San Bernardino would begin with the locale waking up to the sound of alarm clocks or the rising sun. Mothers would ready their young ones, putting on the kettle and emptying the cereal box in the bowl of milk. The bachelors wouldn't have the privilege of having breakfast with their families. So, they would grab a quick bite at the local diners or cafés and then head over to their universities or to their place of employment.

The city's hustle was defined by its standard state economy, consisting of the manufacturing industry, logistics, and transportation, with the National Orange Show, an annual event celebrating the citrus industry, being the city's biggest tourist attraction. The middle class would commute to factories, offices, or retail establishments and make the best out of the provided resources.

During the lunch break, workers would unpack and devour the home-cooked food they had brought with them, or visit local restaurants, cafes, or food trucks and eat while socializing with their colleagues. This would give them a much needed break from their work responsibilities. In the afternoon, businesses and schools would continue their operations, while some people would run errands, and the ladies would stroll to the shopping opportunities San Bernadino's downtown offered. As the day transitioned into the evening, the working class would wind up their work and make their way to the city's transportation facilities. The kind people who worked during the night, providing their experience in the medical field, as well as those working as night guards, would do the opposite and commute to their respective shifts. The nightlife scene in San Bernadino in the year 1974 was, to put simply, modest. Clubs, bars, and lounges were the places where people would go to unwind, dance, and enjoy their peace. As the nights grew late, people would head home to their families or awaiting pets in their small to mid-sized apartments, concluding their day.

There they would spend time with their loved ones, stretch, or engage in personal hobbies like reading, but eventually, all of them would retire to bed, might or might not be planning the next day's activities.

In those days and even now, San Bernardino has had a diverse population, with residents having various ethnic backgrounds. The suburb I used to live in, specifically Rialto, housed a predominantly African American population. Rialto was nicknamed "Hub City" since it was a mix of predominantly African Americans, middle and upper class families.

The city had seen growth in its population after the Second World War had ended. By the year 1970, San Bernardino was home to approximately 120,000 individuals. Like many American cities, San Bernardino faced a fair share of its challenges. Urban Decay, Crime, and Racial Segregation were perhaps the city's biggest challenges. The entire suburb of Rialto was conspicuous of the racial segregation in San Bernardino County. The housing patterns demonstrated a human's status in life. I wouldn't name any names that were responsible for this segregation because it is not the manifesto of this book, but you knew that certain communities living inside of certain housing projects had unequal access to resources and opportunities. Those communities were deliberately sidelined and put into those housing projects as a preemptive measure. Racial discrimination and prejudice were prevalent in various aspects of life. Minority groups, particularly African

Americans, often faced discrimination in employment, education, and they weren't promoted up the ranks in public services. The people that were actually elected in civil service roles and public administrative positions were blinded by racial biases and stereotypes that influenced their interactions and decision making processes. Thankfully San Bernardino, like many cities across the United States, had community organizations. These organizations, civil rights groups, and activists worked tirelessly to address racial inequalities and promote social justice. These groups played an integral role in uplifting minorities from extreme depravity. They battled discrimination and hardly missed an opportunity to raise awareness about the racial impediments in San Bernardino County as well as other states in America. Though no one with an accredited degree in sociology, political science, and anthropology can pinpoint a single reason that caused the three biggest challenges in San Bernardino, one common denominator among them was the economic crisis. The economic crisis people saw around themselves pushed them into a state of turmoil, leading them to stay unoccupied for long periods of time. And I assume you know what happens when we have too much time on our hands.

Back to my story: it was a perfectly average Monday

afternoon in Rialto, San Bernardino. People were likely gravitating towards the food trucks and restaurants, considering it was recess time. I was in our home along with my 9 months old brother and our lovely mum. She was just the most ethereal creation I had seen. She was just the perfect height as she stood at five foot five feet tall. Her figure was thin, and she had the healthiest, long, and wavy hair.

Her body emitted a sort of generous warmth. I couldn't really understand what it was or why it was. I supposed that it was a gift bestowed on her by the Lord. I never thought that a mere mortal could be averse to the side effects of age until I saw my mother. She looked like a teenager – a girl in her mid 20s. My mother had somehow forgotten to age; at least, that is what I believed for the time I had been with her and stayed with her in our little but peaceful apartment. I was so occupied and lost in describing her that I have just realized that I had forgotten to tell you her name. I apologize.

My mother was known to this world as Lashanay Lee. She was born to Frank Hatch. Besides her enchanting beauty, Lashanay never gave the impression that she was a mother after all. She appeared so young for her age that her friends and relatives found it hard to believe she had given birth to five children, including me.

Both my parents' extended families were connected to the Royal Lineage in the United Kingdom. It baffles me when I think about what happened to me, considering that my father's and mother's immediate and distant families were connected to Hollywood royalty and Political Dynasties in the United States. It is impossible for me to process why I had to go through so many challenges when I could've lived a majestic way of life similar to that of a princess.

My parents had gone through a divorce, and the custody of my brother and I were handed to my mother. She was not a working mother but a homemaker who stayed at her home, raising her children and ensuring that they became the best of human beings. Why didn't she work, you might ask. It was because she didn't have to. She had more than enough balance at her bank thanks to the trust fund. Her late father, Frank Hatch a trust fund allocated to her name. Despite her father passing away before my mother was born, he still managed to provide support throughout her life by establishing a trust account in her name – a trust account that was supposed to change my life. Frank Hatch died on his job due to a workplace injury involving a faulty telephone wire, leaving his wife and his unborn child left alone.

The day when my childhood was abruptly taken away from me occurred sometime in the month of April. On the perfectly average afternoon of Monday, Lashanay Lee, my mother, was in the kitchen, extending her hands towards the cabinet to grab the apron. She was planning to cook us a light meal when suddenly a knock was heard on our door, which was shortly followed by a plea for help. Lasha rushed to attend the door, finding her good friend standing anxiously on the other side. She had come to our door seeking help, lamenting that her husband was abusing her. You could say that my mother was an altruist; she would offer a helping hand to almost anybody. Without hesitation, she grabbed the keys to our apartment, locked my brother and me inside, and hurriedly rushed to assist her friend. Little did the pure soul know this was a trap set by someone we would later know about to snatch my brother and me away from her. Seeing her lock, us inside, a nosey neighbor called the police and social services. This devilish plan was purposefully schemed out to paint Lasha as a neglectful mother. One thing led to another, and Lasha was denied custody of her own creations. In April of 1976, I, known in the context of this book as Willow, was placed in foster care alongside my nine-month old brother…

Chapter 2 –
Adjusting to New Adoptive Family

They snatched me from my mother like I was nothing but a commodity. Yet, they say that animals are worse. Well at least a sow doesn't abandon its cub until it has fully grown or learned the survival skills. A tigress would kill the predator or do her best to deny the custody of her cub to humans. A fox would rally her species at the very least to ensure that her younger stays protected and not taken away from her. Yet, it often said that animals are dealt with a worse hand.

I was taken away from my loving mother without a proper explanation. In my moments of reflection, I have come to accept my fate because I couldn't possibly ask any questions or perhaps exercise my right to seek an explanation, as I was too young. If we are being honest with ourselves, what could I have asked the social services workers? I was a three-year-old girl, elder to a nine months' infant. All I could do was cry and pray that everything would be alright soon.

Staying in the child welfare office for a short while, I was introduced to my new adoptive family. I was dumbfounded by the brightness inside of the welfare office, but not in a pleasant way. It appeared to me that all the city's lights were installed inside of that office building because it was so bright from the inside. I was told to sit at an empty bench and wait for my grandfather. I remained seated patiently on the bench while my younger brother sucked on his thumb and observed everyone around him from his tiny crib. A while had gone by and there was no sign of my grandfather. My back was paining from sitting upright all this time, and I could really use some sleep or perhaps a few minutes to rest and lie on my back. I hesitantly stood up to take a look at the building's door, hoping that grandpa had arrived. When I couldn't see the sight of him, I decided to lie down on the bench. There was a metal cabinet handing right above the bench, so I had to be careful not to hit my head when I lay down. It didn't take me much long to drift off to sleep. I used my left hand as the pillow, found a comfortable position, and let myself drift away into sleep.

I had slept for half an hour when my grandfather arrived into the welfare office and woke me up. I woke up with a funny face and rubbed my eyes as grandfather briefed me about our transfer to a new home. It was hard to make sense of whatever was happening but I had no other option but to follow whatever I was being told. In those adverse times, I had to mature beyond my years and develop a sense of maturity that surpassed my age. My grandfather signed some important documents and orchestrated the adoption of Willow and my infant brother by a couple who lived just a few houses down. They were friends of the family, particularly the husband, who had familial connections to my mother's side.

The moment I laid eyes on my adoptive mother, I felt a glimmer of hope. The woman had a nurturing aura about her. During my conversation with grandpa that day, he told me that my new mother is a nice lady. He told me that she had fostered kids for many years, and some of them had grown up to become remarkably successful and valuable contributors to society. My soon to be mother's previous experience in adopting children gave my grandfather a sense of reassurance. With a bachelor's and master's degree, and having served as a preschool director, she seemed like the perfect match to care for the young Willow and her tiny brother.

The two of us settled into our new residence, which stood out with its larger size compared to the typical suburban homes. Besides us, there were other children residing in this house, the newly added members of our extended family. While I wasn't accustomed to sharing my living space with kids other than my brother, having my own room felt like a true blessing. It afforded me the solitude I needed to process all that I had experienced, filling me with optimism about my fresh start.

In the beginning, everything seemed perfect. My new family made sure all our needs were met, ensuring that my brother and I were well-fed and attended school and church regularly. Every now and then, the couple would treat us to ice cream and candies, and they even allowed me to stay up late at night so I could watch something on TV. She was skilled in sewing, and during her free time, she would craft clothes for me to wear to school or church.

When I reached the age of eight (or ten, pardon my memory), there were occasional days when I would head to school after getting ready at my grandparents' house. My grandmother would lovingly prepare my breakfast and carefully comb my hair. Afterward, with my books and stationery neatly stowed in my small bag, I would set off for school alongside my cousin Dayton, who was of the same age as me. We enjoyed each other's company during those walks. Upon returning to my grandparents' home, we would share a dinner together, and then my foster mother would arrive to pick me up. I share this small anecdote to convey that I had embraced my foster parent as a cherished member of my family, just as Dayton and my grandparents had done.

Hard to believe it now, but at the time, I couldn't help but believe that I had finally found a place where I truly belonged.

Yet, as the days turned into months and months turn to years, I began to notice a disturbing change in my adoptive mother's behavior. The warmth that once enveloped my first adoptive mother's home seemed to fade away like a distant memory. It started with simple requests, but they soon escalated into unreasonable demands. I was growing older and starting to realize that it was better for me to keep a distance from my adolescence. But, one cannot deny nature or its process; I was growing older and my adoptive family's behavior was shifting from when they first welcomed me into their house.

I found myself thrust into a new role—one of a servant rather than a cherished family member. While other children my age were free to enjoy the carefree perks of youth, I was burdened with household chores and responsibilities beyond my formative years. The look from the outside of our window was depressing. I was seeing kids my age laughing and playing along while I was left to scrub dishes and sweep floors. My small hands calloused and my spirit was weary.

After years of contemplation, I have finally uncovered the reason my adoptive mother's lack of affection towards me. My adoptive mother, though trained to raise a child, seemed to lack the nurturing instinct of a true mother. She approached her role with an extreme professionalism. She focused on the practical aspects of caregiving rather than forming a genuine emotional connection with us siblings. It would have been nice if she wasn't so professional and talked to me like a mother does with her child. It would be nice if she had combed my hair once a while. This emotional distance only deepened the sense of isolation that I felt within this home.

It was a bitter pill for Willow to swallow, witnessing her peers being showered with love and attention while she and her brother were left to navigate the lonely corridors of neglect. The vibrant laughter and playful chatter from neighboring houses served as a constant reminder of the childhood joys that seemed forever out of their reach.

The burden of household duties stunted my growth. My young shoulders were carrying more than I could handle. I was robbed of the carefree innocence that should have accompanied my formative years. While other children danced through life, I carefully balanced my duties with the longing for a childhood I could only dream of.

The absence of a genuine connection with my adoptive mother added another layer of hardship to my plight. I missed my mother all the more. When I was all alone, I would think about her and wonder where she was and if she would ever come and rescue me. My heart yearned for the warmth of a mother's love, the nurturing embrace that would assure that I belonged in this world. Instead of reassurance, I was met with distant gazes and cool detachment, leaving an indelible mark on my young soul.

As the time progressed, my resilience began to waver under the weight of my responsibilities and the emotional neglect I endured. My adoptive mother was now expecting me to fetch her meals besides the routine house chores as washing the dishes and sweeping the floor.

Since the work was too much and I was under the weather, I decided to bail on work and sleep peacefully this one night. Funny enough, this was the night when my adoptive mother's dissatisfaction reached a boiling point. She stormed into my room with fury in her eyes, her voice venomous and laced with anger. She awakened me in the middle of night, grabbed my shoulders and demand that I clean the forgotten dishes still lying in the sink. Before I could comprehend what was happening, I found myself in the midst of a violent confrontation.

In the darkness, fear mingled with adrenaline, transforming me into a fierce protector of my own well-being. It was as if a ghost had possessed me as I fought back against my mother with a strength I didn't know I possessed. In the midst of chaos, I did something that I regret to this day. I accidently broke my adoptive mother's arm, hearing the cracking sound in that silent room as clear as a thunderstorm on a rainy night. Both of us were taken aback by the event that had transpired. It felt as though the ground had been abruptly taken away from beneath our collective feet, casting a shadow over our once promising relationship.

This pivotal incident marked the beginning of a new chapter in Willow's life. The consequences of her actions reverberated far beyond the confines of her adoptive home. Little did I know that this fracture would lead to the entrance of Livera, a mysterious figure who would play an integral role in the next phase of my journey.

I was taken to the child services office once again and knew that I wouldn't return to the woman that I once considered my new mother. I knew that a new character will be introduced in the story of my life and I just prayed that she would be nicer than the woman with a broken hand. As I faced the heart-wrenching reality of being separated from a woman that raised me from the age of three until thirteen, I found myself closer to entering a foster care home that offered little solace. The once-familiar comforts of stability were replaced with uncertainty and trepidation. It was in this unfamiliar terrain that I was required to summon my resilience and draw upon the strength that lay dormant within her.

I thin, average looking woman introduced herself as "Liveria." She promised that she would be nice to me; well at least, she believed so. She offered me freedom but I was once again too naïve to understand that it would come at a cost.

Living with Livera and the cost I had to pay is a story for another chapter.

Chapter 3 –

New home but abysmal life

I sat on the same bench when I was first brought inside of that child welfare building after I was taken away from my mother warm lap. As I sat there wondering about my immediate future, all the memories of the time I spend with my mother came rushing back. I remember how she bathed us as we played with the bubbles in our little bath tub. She would cup her hands and fill them with small floating bubbles and then place them on my head. She would then say, "You are my princess and I have made you wear a crown!" Those days were the happiest I had been. I would often playfully throw some water on my mum while she was bathing us. My little brother couldn't understand what was going on so he would simply laugh and giggle while sitting in his baby chair, watching mum and I play with suds and water.

She would cook us the breakfast everyone in our suburban town would kill to eat. It had every nutrition, from protein to carbs, but unlike most healthy meals, our breakfast was rich in taste. The eggs were nicely cooked and the bacon was never fully fired, making it crispy but not burned. In the evening, my mother would read us books that her mother had read to her when she was a child. I would get immersed in the world that those fictional tales created. If the story's main character was a young girl, waiting to be rescued by her lover, I would instantly draw comparison between that girl and me. I would think that my lover would come someday but instead of running away with him, I would sway him to live with me, my brother, and my mum. I didn't want to be rescued because I loved my mother and the relationship we shared and nothing would inspire me to leave her. Come to think of it, my mother was reading me princely rescue adventures because she knew that there would be a time when I needed rescuing. She knew that there would be a time when I had to throw away everything and run.

As I fondly reminisced about the joyous moments spent with my mother, a sudden, harsh shout jolted me back to reality. "Boy, I ain't your real mama, so you better behave, or you can spend the rest of your meaningful life in some other place!" These words were hurled by a woman in her early forties, her frustration evident as she scolded her adopted son in the presence of social services officers. In an instant, my thoughts were yanked away from the heavenly memories I had been floating in.

I shifted my attention to the surroundings of the social services building, scrutinizing it carefully. The interior of the office exuded a stark and clinical atmosphere, amplifying Willow's sense of unease and displacement. I settled onto an uncomfortable plastic chair, stealing a glance at Charlotte Gideon's injured arm. I never had any intention of causing her harm, but amidst the turmoil of that fateful night, my actions had unforeseen consequences.

The counselor in the child welfare office kept on dialing numbers on his telephone and the employees were reading newspapers with their legs resting at the top of their tables. A small group of people, likely workers at the child services, engaged in gossiping about their colleagues while a three-person line was formed at the coffee station. Each three of them had big stomach and were slowly growing impatient of the coffee machine's troubles with pouring the hot and black liquid at a slow rate.

My astute observation of the child welfare was broken shortly after I saw a familiar face. A Caucasian woman with blonde hair walked into the child services office alongside her husband. I knew I had seen that face before but couldn't figure out where. A sparkle on her right hand, caused by the ever so many lights inside the office building caught my attention. She was wearing those Ichthy bracelets; one made of tiny marbles or gemstones with a cross sign at the middle. I instantly recognized her. She was Livera Dana, a friend of my mother and a fellow church goer.

Livera Dana, a Caucasian woman, graced the scene with her slender frame, fair complexion, and flowing blonde locks. Her height was typical for a woman, and her presence exuded an aura of self-assured confidence that naturally captured attention and commanded respect. But Livera's physical attributes were only a fraction of her persona. Beneath her meticulously groomed exterior, her mind was as sharp as a blade, and her heart harbored secrets and deception. Livera possessed an astonishing knack for adapting her demeanor to suit any given situation, effortlessly shifting from warm and empathetic to cool and calculated as circumstances dictated. As she entered the building, her polished appearance and inviting smile concealed the hidden motives lurking beneath the surface. Livera had earned a reputation for finding new homes for troubled children, and she held a particular interest in my case.

Livera approached Willow, her voice laced with empathy as she spoke. She offered an explanation for Charlotte's behavior. She blamed Charlotte's awful behavior on her advanced age. Livera explained that Charlotte was old and it had strained her ability to care for a child. She explained that due to Charlotte's advanced age, she had placed all the responsibilities and duties of the house on my young shoulders. I couldn't see through the baloney she was uttering, so my naïve thirteen-year-old self believed every word she said. At the time and given my situation at Charlotte's house, Livera was actually making a lot of sense.

The good woman, Charlotte Gideon had grown past her best years and even I was perceiving her as burden although I was guest or sort of a pilgrim residing in her property.

When Livera realized that I was blown away by her revelation, she smartly painted a picture of a life filled with freedom, independence, and the luxuries that every teenager dreams of.

She promised me the opportunity to wear any clothes I desired, go to parties, and experience the kind of freedom that had been denied to me before. Livera enticed me with a tantalizing vision of a life beyond the confinements of my current situation. She was making all these promises and it made my eyes sparkle with a mixture of hope and longing, yearning for a taste of the life that I had always imagined.

Livera masterfully highlighted the obvious difference between my past and the seemingly bright possibilities she could offer. She painted a picture of a life where I would have control over my own choices, where I could freely express myself and embrace the independence I longed for. My mind had started to concoct the perfect life of an ordinary girl. I was beginning to think that these years of struggle would be the perfect plot to my autobiography that I would now write inside of the comfy walls of Livera's house. I was thinking that this would finally be my artistic break that I desperately needed. Livera's words resonated deeply with my vulnerable heart, fueling a flicker of hope that maybe, just maybe, this could be the fresh start I desperately needed.

Driven by that yearning for acceptance and freedom, I made the fateful decision to move in with Livera. In the beginning, her demeanor remained pleasant, her promises dangling enticingly before me like shimmering mirages in a desert. But as time passed, I realized that those promises were nothing more than illusions, skillfully crafted to lure me into her trap.

Gradually, the mask of kindness began to slip from Livera's face, revealing the true nature of her intentions. The once generous and caring facade she had presented started to crumble, leaving behind a void of unfulfilled assurances. The freedom she had promised me turned into a cage, confining my spirit and suffocating my dreams.

It became painfully clear that Livera had no intention of delivering on her promises. Her words were nothing but empty echoes, her actions were almost mocking the vibrant life she had painted for me. The more I tried to hold onto the fragments of hope she had instilled within me, the more they slipped through my fingers, leaving behind a bitter taste of disappointment and betrayal.

I found myself ensnared in Livera's web of manipulation, her calculated maneuvers rendering me powerless and eroding my self-worth. The more I yearned for the acceptance and love I so desperately needed, the tighter she clung to her control over my life, relishing in her dominance.

Once again, I was relegated to the role of a housekeeper, tasked with washing dishes, doing laundry, and sweeping the floors of her house. However, this time, my brother and I were treated even worse than second-class citizens. In addition to the daily chores she burdened me with, Livera imposed a relentless spring cleaning regimen upon me. Without any consideration for the vulnerability of a fourteen-year-old, unacknowledged orphan, she compelled me to scrub her cabinets, dust her walls and baseboards, clean and restock the refrigerator and pantry, and take out the garbage every night before bedtime.

She had such a suffocating grasp on my moving that I had to ask for her permission even if I had to use the bathroom. For me the bathroom was a comforting place because I could go there and cry without the fear of unwanted attention.

As my fourteenth birthday turned to sixteen, the freedom Livera had offered became a mere illusion. The true nature of her intentions was revealed and I was angry at the choices I made in my life. It was evident that the allure of wealth and control had blinded Livera to the needs and well-being of the child she had taken under her wing.

Rather than treating Willow as a beloved child, Livera treated her as a pawn in her quest for power and financial gain. The promises of freedom and autonomy transformed into a suffocating prison, where every move I made was scrutinized and controlled. It seemed like all my own needs had vanished into thin air. It was as if us siblings were invisible, relegated to the status of second- class citizens within the walls they called home.

Livera's greed knew no bounds. As I approached my eighteenth birthday, a time that should have been filled with excitement and anticipation, Livera began demanding that I pay her rent on a monthly basis. I was shocked and confused. Growing up at Charlotte Gideon and Livera's house, I had always believed that the social services department was affiliated with the State and was providing monthly stipends to Livera to take care of my expenses. The realization that the woman who had the statue of my mother had been exploiting my trust fund hit me like a dagger to the heart.

In a daze, I made my way to the authorities, seeking answers and clarity about my trust fund. My trembling hands clutched the last remnants of hope as I approached the counter. But my hopes were shattered as the truth was unveiled before my eyes. My trust fund, meant to secure my future and well-being, was empty. A mixture of anger, betrayal, and despair swirled within me as I realized that I had been deceived, manipulated, and robbed of my rightful inheritance. The very system that was supposed to protect me had failed me. In that moment, the world seemed cruel and unforgiving.

As I reflect upon those days, I can't help but wonder how I allowed myself to be so easily deceived. But deep down, I know that my longing for a better life clouded my judgment, blinding me to the true nature of the person I had trusted. The once alluring promise of freedom had transformed into a harsh reality, and I was left with the painful realization that I had exchanged one form of captivity for another.

And so, I began to question everything. The social services department, the monthly stipends I assumed were for my well-being, and even the trust fund that had been entrusted to Livera. The decision to confront the authorities and inquire about the truth was a hopeful one. I was hoping that I could take all the funds with me and run off to somewhere kinder in this world, along with my young brother. Little did I know that the journey to uncover the truth would lead me to a devastating revelation - my trust fund, my lifeline, was nothing more than an empty void.

Chapter 4 –

18 and Making Moves

The man attending the counter of Trustee services informed me that the account under my name was empty. I asked him to check again and even called out the syllables of my name. I refused to surrender my hope as I believed that all the suffering I had endured up until that point was to build my character. I believed that I was taken away from my mother and forced to perform menial tasks such as wiping the floors and cleaning the dishes so I could be better prepared for the responsibilities of adulthood. I thought that all the unpaid labor I was subjected to would eventually pay off, making me more responsible and mature enough to handle the trust fund that awaited me. However, the ground beneath my feet was suddenly ripped away when the man on the counter announced that he had rechecked my trust account and was certain that it didn't contain any monies.

It was devastating, to say the least. My shoulders drooped as I turned around and made the painful walk back to Livera's energy-sapping house. I remember that unfortunate evening as vividly as if it had happened yesterday. It was raining heavily and now that I think about it, it was extremely fortunate that it was raining massively that evening. I was able to walk back to Livera's house, soaked from head to toe and no one could have seen me crying. It was a blessing in disguise.

My heart sank as I walked through the front door of Livera's house, the weight of the devastating truth heavy upon my shoulders. I stood still for a while, contemplating my next move. For a moment I thought of running away and never seeing the sight of Livera or her house again. Although my life had shaped me into a person who was more mature for her age, the truth was that I was still an eighteen year old teenager. My instincts were that of a teenager and the thoughts in my mind reeked irrationality. On the thought of running away forever, I believed it was possible for me to survive in a homeless shelter. The stories my biological mother had read me during my childhood years had a more profound impact than I anticipated. It made me perceive fantasy as something plausible in the world that I and everyone around me lived in. I was convinced, in that moment, that a prince would come to my rescue and take me away from the homeless person's house.

As I stood outside, soaked on the porch of her house, planning my escape from the intangible cage I was confined in, God's wisdom struck me. I realized that I was an undeclared orphan in one of the most politically volatile cities of America. A vulnerable young adult like me would be preyed on by the men like vulture feeds on dead birds and other animal carcass. God's wisdom also made me realize that I was alone in this journey and I had a brother to look after. So, as the drowning-in-despair version of myself, I walked inside Livera's house, feeling disappointed.

Livera, always quick to seize any opportunity to exert control, greeted me with a cold and calculating stare. There was no sympathy or remorse in her eyes, only a sense of satisfaction knowing that she had me right where she wanted me. With an unnerving smile, she wasted no time in making her demands known.

"Now that you've seen your trust fund and the fact that you're eighteen, Willow, it's time for you to contribute to the household," she declared, her voice dripping with a mix of entitlement and superiority. "If you want to continue living under my roof, you'll need to pay me monthly rent."

"And, it shouldn't be late. I expect the payment on fifth of every month at the earliest." She declared.

Her words felt like a dagger to my already wounded heart. I had hoped for compassion, for understanding in my time of need, but Livera saw this as an opportunity to exploit my vulnerability. She knew that I had graduated and would now have more time to work, no longer occupied with the demands of studying. She knew that I was on the cusp of adulthood, legally able to earn a living. And she knew just how to use that against me.

The dream of pursuing internships, of gaining experience in fields that fascinated me like any other teenager my age, was cruelly snatched away. The pressure to pay rent loomed over me like a dark cloud, forcing me into a desperate scramble for any job that paid enough to meet Livera's demands. I had no choice but to settle for odd jobs that consumed large chunks of my day, leaving little room for personal growth or exploring my true passions.

While the teenager I had graduated with reveled in the joys of youth, seizing opportunities and embracing the excitement of new experiences, I found myself trapped in a cycle of survival. The dreams I once held dear became distant echoes, drowned out by the relentless demands of adulthood thrust upon me too soon. In the morning, I would walk the pets of the neighborhood residents, then in the midday, I would involve myself in yard work, maintaining lawns, mowing grass, and raking leaves. For the evening, I found myself a job at a car wash facility. My role there involved cleaning the exteriors and interiors of cars.

Depending on the package the customer had chosen, I would also detail their vehicles using the equipment and chemicals provided by the shop owner. The three odd jobs I took on allowed me to earn just enough cash to afford a room under Livera's roof for both me and my brother. For an extra source of income, I offered babysitting services every weekend to the people in my neighborhood.

I was paying her rent on time but still Livera was blinded by her power.

She still wanted control over my every move. The psychological abuse I endured under her roof grew worse with each passing day. She relished in belittling my aspirations, reminding me of my worthlessness whenever I dared to question her authority. She took pleasure in the awareness that I had no alternative but to remain under her roof, trapped in a struggle for my own survival. There were times when I couldn't differentiate between my supposed adoptive mother and a psychopath. She wouldn't show an ounce of empathy for the work I was doing in order to keep a roof over our heads. After witnessing her true colors for over four years, I didn't expect her to treat me like her own daughter, but I had hoped that she would at least respect the hard work I was putting in.

Accepting that my world was unjust, I toiled day in and day out, my spirit crushed but my determination unwavering. I took on odd jobs that paid more, sacrificing my time and energy just to meet the mounting rent demands. The weight of my responsibilities threatened to break me, but I refused to let Livera Dana's manipulation define my worth.

I had accepted my fate but the case of millions disappearing in my trust fund intrigued my curiosity for eternity. There was so much going on in my life at the time that I couldn't find the time to investigate the disappearing act of funds in my trust account. On second thought, it wouldn't be wrong to assume that Livera had intentionally made me engaged with the house chores and working so many odd jobs so I couldn't find the time to find out the truth.

A few years later when I had moved away from Livera I finally got the chance to uncover the truth about my trust fund. I asked around and discovered that I had indeed been defrauded by the woman who came into my life disguised as my second (or third) mother.

Livera and her husband utilized a portion of the trust fund money without notifying me. They allocated these funds for an out-of-town business venture and the purchase of luxury cars. Unbeknownst to me, I thought that my money was safely guarded and untouched inside of my trust fund. A few months later of my eighteenth birthday, I intended to withdraw some money for my senior prom expenses. I was successful in withdrawing money that day, and I was told that the remaining amount was scheduled to be released upon my graduation and my twentieth birthday. This was before I went to the trust services offices to withdraw all of my money and run away from Livera.

The folks at the Department of Trust Funds had assured me that I would rightfully inherit my trust fund on my twentieth birthday. However, Livera had other intentions entirely. She seized control of my money, disguising her million-dollar windfall as a settlement from a car accident dating back to 1990. This elaborate deception eventually unraveled, exposing that the million dollars had actually originated from the trust fund.

Livera and her husband had concealed this truth due to the appearance of 40 million dollars as unclaimed property, which, under the law, could be utilized by the foster agency for municipal and city purposes if the rightful owner failed to claim it after a two-year period.

When the reality of my trust fund's misappropriation

finally came to light, I couldn't help but feel a deep sense of disappointment. Not because of the loss of wealth, but because, despite Livera's cruelty, I had still considered her my mother. I had placed my utmost trust in her, and the ideathat a mother could defraud her own child had never crossedmy mind.

This heartless and illegal act against a child exiting the system, as well as her biological family, remains a perplexing mystery. Due to the statute of limitations having been reached, the full truth will likely never be unveiled. The case file, which contained a wealth of evidence, has been destroyed, with a follow-up letter indicating that even with legal representation, the file is permanently sealed.

Since that day, I vowed to keep fighting, to find a way out of this suffocating existence and discover a life where I could thrive on my own terms. I refused to let this betrayal define my future or hinder my aspirations. As the next chapters in my life unfolded, I remained resolute. I forged my own path, guided by integrity, authenticity, and an unwavering pursuit of my dreams. I embraced the challenges that lay ahead. I knew that my journey would be marked by ups and downs, but the struggles in my life had taught me the skill to overcome any obstacle. With a heart full of resilience, I embarked on an extraordinary journey of self-discovery, determined to create a life that was truly my own.

Chapter 5 –

This Girl is in her Twenties!

Though I had promised myself that I wouldn't allow this betrayal, this fraud, and this cruelty to hinder my aspirations, I was only humans and could only suppress my emotions for so long. All the emotions a human possess stuck me at the same time as I realized that I was broke and had no value or possession that I could call property. I couldn't claim ownership of a piece of land or a vehicle; those were the first two things I thought of buying when I would be given access to my trust fund. The revelation of the embezzlement of my trust fund sent shockwaves through my soul.

I mentioned in the previous chapter that I conducted an independent investigation about the vanishing of my trust fund. I discovered that Livera had stolen and squandered my grandfather's fortune, using all of that money to buy luxurious cars for her and her husband and also investing in out of town business ventures. Well, to add salt to my wounds, I found out that those business she had invested in were related to music and entertainment industry. I will leave to your imagination to decide what that "Entertainment" businesses were.

Of course she couldn't have done this on her own; she needed accomplices that would guide her in every step of the way. Unfortunately for me, I couldn't catch their names or locations, despite knowing that a number of influential people having connections all over the States were involved in this defraud. Without their connections and expertise, Livera was too dumb to orchestrate such a heinous con. My guess is: they were promised huge sums from my trust fund, given that they could grant Livera an access to it. It is obvious that they were successful in affording her access to my trust fund. It wouldn't be unreasonable to believe that she might have paid them off as soon as she was able to access the money in my trust fund. The last thing I know regarding this case is the people involved, excluding Livera and her husband, moved out of the state and opened businesses that could not be linked or traced back to this trust fund embezzlement. Having fled the state, these collaborators left behind a trail of shattered dreams and stolen promises for me.

With my trust fund reduced to nothing but a memory, I found myself in a dire situation. It was then that Livera's daughter-in-law, Searedlina Dana, made a seemingly generous offer for me to stay with her. This offer came out of nowhere. I was bearing Livera's inhumane treatment alone and I never shared my grievances with Searedlina. So how did she comprehend that I was suffering and offered me residence at her place? Well, she didn't take much time to show her real colors and make apparent her ulterior motives. Searedlina required me to pay a monthly rent of $150, soon after I moved in with her. I was already burdened with the loss of fortune that my grandfather and parents had accumulated and I was supposed to go back to doing odd jobs to ensure that there was a roof over me and my brother's head.

Searedlina's living arrangements were far from ideal. She only had a small two-bedroom apartment, and the limited space meant that I was given a rollaway bed to sleep in, often placed in the hallway. The lack of privacy and comfort was a constant reminder of my diminished status in her home. The state of my living resembled that of a malnourished bird, having to live and survive on meager crumbs. It is worth mentioning that the rollaway bed had passed its prime years and was reduced to a thick cotton sheet due to deterioration from excessive use. So, in a way, I was actually hurting my back sleeping on that thick sheet of cloth that Searedlina considered a bed.

Adding to the complexity of my situation with Livera and her daughter in law, tragedy had struck the Dana family not long before I moved in with Searedlina. I was a graduate in the year 1992 but still remember that day for an unforeseen event. In the year 1992, during a UCLA retreat that was meant to inspire young minds to pursue higher education, news of Nicholas Dana's untimely death shattered the joyous atmosphere. The loss of Searedlina's husband cast a dark cloud over the family, leaving them in a state of grief and financial instability. The death of Nicholas was both condemnable and a sorrowful state of affairs, but there could've been a silver-lining from the unpleasant situation. I thought that Nicholas's untimely death might just make Livera and her daughter in law a better person. I thought that God had taken away a son and a husband to teach His distracted creations a lesson. A lesson that implied life is as soft and fragile as a bubble, meaning that it could be snatched away in a blink of an eye. Although I had little hopes from Livera, I believed that Searedlina could change. She would understand that there is life after death where she must be answerable to our Lord. With the unfortunate passing away of her husband, I believed she would repent and cease scamming me like her mother in law and finally show some mercy. Maybe she could even speak with her mother in law and condemn her wicked and exploitative ways. The least I expected was Searedlina finally showing me some love and care like she was my big sister. Sadly none of what I had anticipated happened.

Instead of considering the intricacies of the life that is given to us or remembering her husband in retrospection, Searedlina wasted no time in expressing her expectations. She made it clear that she needed a consistent stream of income, and she looked to me to provide it. The $150 monthly rent was just the beginning. It was apparent that she desired more, as if she saw me as the solution to her financial woes, no that her husband was no longer the breadwinner of her house. I could sense her longing for someone who would not only cover their rent but also take care of her bills and necessities, effectively making me the breadwinner of the household.

The prospect of becoming entangled in Searedlina's desperate need for financial support filled me with dread. It was clear that she expected far more than what I could afford. Her living standards were questionable, and it seemed as though she desired a tenant who would shoulder the burden of her responsibilities, on top of fulfilling their own obligations.

I found myself at a crossroads, trapped between the relentless demands of my circumstances. Searedlina was not in the mood of working any jobs herself. The apartment in which we were housed was owned under her name and that fact somehow gave her a leverage over me. I was naïve and not mature enough to search for another foster parent on my own. I had been a witness to the exhausting process of being assigned to foster parents and I knew I did not have resilience in me to sit through the process of filling papers, signing off things, and worst of all, waiting.

So the likelihood of shifting elsewhere was off the table, meaning that the weight of financial obligations of a grown up woman who was suddenly behaving like a child began threating my aspiration and to suffocate my dreams. Like the teenagers my age, I yearned for a chance to explore my passions, to chase after the opportunities that would allow me to flourish. I had already graduated high school by the time I was living with Searedlina, but like every girl my age, I had great ambitions of joining a reputable college to peruse higher education. You see, from a very young age I was curious to learning. You could lock me inside of a library and I wouldn't complain, such was my passion for learning. Nevertheless, my circumstances were hell bent on pushing me away from studies. The reality that lay in front of me was stark—I had to prioritize survival, even if it meant sacrificing my own desires.

As the days turned into weeks, and the weeks into months, I juggled odd jobs and exhausting work schedules to meet Searedlina's demands. I became the sole provider in a household that was drowning in grief and desperation.

The burden of responsibility weighed heavily on my young shoulders, reminding me of the injustices I had endured and the uncertain future that lay ahead.

As I reached my twenties, I found myself liberated from the clutches of Searedlina's demanding grip. I had mustered the courage to leave her house behind, seeking refuge with my adoptive sister, Ralea Hines. Ralea was one of the kindest person I had seen in my life. She was always ready to lend a helping hand. She went above and beyond to support me, providing for my needs and even spoiling me with things I had never experienced before. From buying me my first car to ensuring I had proper clothes and food, Ralea's unwavering support brought a newfound joy and stability into my life. She even encouraged me to pursue higher education, assuring me that it would open doors to financial security.

Live was suddenly easier with Ralea around as I felt a renewed sense of happiness and optimism. The end of the tunnel was finally looking bright and it felt as if I was closer to the tunnel's end rather than being at the starting point.

Ralea's calming personality brought a sense of warmth and belonging, reminding me that family could be chosen and that love could mend the wounds inflicted by a tumultuous past.

In my twenties, I experienced the highs and lows of romantic relationships. I had recently ended a promising relationship with Dylan Matlock, a man who treated me like royalty. Despite the long-distance challenges between us, Dylan hardly skipped a chance of making me feel cherished. Dylan was me drug for escapism – he would catapult me away to Los Angeles on weekends to spend time with his family. He was a respectable man with a stable job in construction, and he even owned a stylish car. I envisioned a financially secure future with him. Interestingly, he bore an uncanny resemblance to Tupac Shakur.

But the distance eventually took its toll, and our relationship came to an end. Dylan's mother's interference further complicated matters, creating a rift between us. Despite the breakup, I couldn't help but think of him and wonder what could have been. The memories we shared, the love we had cultivated, lingered in my heart, refusing to be forgotten.

One fateful night, while out with my girlfriends at a bar, I caught a glimpse of a man who bore a striking resemblance to Dylan. My heart skipped a beat as memories flooded back, and I couldn't shake the feeling of longing that washed over me. In that moment, I made up my mind—I would reach out to Dylan, express my thoughts and emotions, and see if there was still a chance for us.

Getting his address was an obstacle. In an old conversation he had shared the news of his moving but I had forgotten to ask for his new address.

Thankfully I remembered the address of his mother's house. So without thinking further I penned a heartfelt letter, pouring out my feelings and recounting the moments we had shared. I entrusted the letter to the postal service, hoping that it would find its way to Dylan's mother's residence.

Days turned into weeks, and anticipation filled my every waking moment.

Then, one day, a call came through to Ralea from none other than Dylan himself. The letter had finally reached him, and he sought me out. Excitement surged through my veins as I learned the news. Although I was at work when he called, the message was delivered, and my heart soared with the prospect of rekindling our relationship.

Summer of '94 marked the beginning of a fresh chapter in our love story. Dylan and I embraced the challenge of a long-distance relationship, with him residing in Los Angeles and me in Rialto. But this time, we were adamant on making the long distance work. I was assured that his mother would not come in our way and keep her business to herself.

The two of us had learned from our past, and our bond grew stronger than ever before. We navigated the distance with grace, nurturing a relationship free from arguments and infidelity. As we spent more time together, we cherished every moment, savoring the joy and love that blossomed between us.

Chapter 6 -
A New Chapter Begins

Valentine's Day of 1995 brought an unexpected turn in my relationship with Dylan. He dropped down on his knees and asked for my hand in marriage. Seeing his right hand extended towards me, his eyes filled with hope and love as he awaited my response, I knew that this man had good intentions. I couldn't help but feel a surge of happiness, but deep down, I knew that marriage wasn't something I was ready for at that moment. I was still very young and had a lot of things on my bucket list that needed to be accomplished. I know that there are plenty of women out there who aren't confined by marriage and have the liberty to do whatever they want. Yet, my conscious at the time made it clear to me that I wouldn't be able to achieve the incredible feats that people I looked up to had achieved. In all of this back and forth between my thought, one thing was perfectly clear; I didn't want to disappoint Dylan. So despite my hesitation, I accepted his proposal without giving an official answer. Our love was strong, but the weight of commitment weighed heavily on my shoulders.

In the months that followed, life had planned for me

another unexpected turn. On a random morning, I woke up feeling uneasy in the stomach. I checked my first aid kit for some painkiller but seeing that it was empty, I decided to schedule an appointment with the doctor later to get a prescription. I was allotted the evening slot so I waited all day for the appointment, lying down on my bed and doing nothing that required physical effort. As the evening approached, something in my room reminded me of Dylan and the intimate encounter we had shared not long ago. I quickly grabbed some cash from my purse and rushed to the corner store. I picked up some pregnancy test strips from the shelves, paid the shopkeeper and returned home. I checked the pregnancy test strip in the bathroom and discovered that I was four weeks pregnant with Dylan's child. Excitement mingled with apprehension as I considered the future that lay ahead.

At this point in life, I was back living with Livera, her husband, and her oldest daughter, Diablotia Dana. I had left Ralea because I realized that she needed space. I felt that she was too occupied with me, making sure that my needs were met and that I was happy. She was the perfect elder sister, providing me with shelter and guidance, acquainting me with the good and bad aspects of life, and doing everything in her power to make my life easier. I could've stayed with her forever and be royally treated but I wasn't selfish. Ralea deserved her space and her own life. She needed to surf on chasing waves, drink the night out with her girlfriends, catch the glimpse of falling stars, and feel the sensation of a lover's touch like every female her age feels. So realizing that I might unintentionally sabotage my foster sister's life, I packed my bags and moved back in with Livera and her family.

I kept the news of my pregnancy a secret to Livera but I didn't think twice before sharing the news with Dylan. He was filled with joy upon learning about my pregnancy, but I couldn't shake the overwhelming uncertainty that plagued my thoughts. Balancing school and work was already challenging, and now the responsibility of motherhood loomed large.

As per our usual routine, I made weekly visits to Dylan, driving alone on the freeway to spend cherished moments together. Dylan was sometimes reckless with his car so the officers would tow his car to an impoundment lot. To meet me when his car was unavailable, Dylan would buy train tickets to my town. Our love transcended the distance, and every encounter reinforced the bond we shared.

During one of my visits to Los Angeles, around the time I was two to three months pregnant, Livera's relentless demands for rent interrupted the tranquility. The two of us had agreed to a new rent agreement. According our arrangement, I would pay the $300 monthly rent upon my return from Los Angeles. However, Livera was single-minded in her attempts to ruin my short vacations to LA. Her endless paging and calls to Ralea made it evident that she was impatient and wanted me to return home so I could pay her the rent. I had tried keeping the news of my pregnancy concealed from Livera for the longest time but one cannot deny the course of nature. My pregnancy was progressing, which meant that the size of my stomach was expanding. Willow was left with no choice but to disclose the news to her foster mother after returning from her visit to Los Angeles. I had anticipated that she and her foster fraud family wouldn't the news of my pregnancy too kindly. Livera, along with the input of her family, disapproved of my decision to keep the baby and urged me to consider an abortion.

Frustration and uncertainty engulfed me, prompting a pivotal decision. I resolved not to return to Livera's house, knowing that she would only complicate matters further. With everything hanging in the balance, I made the bold choice to move to Hollywood with Dylan. He had recently relocated to an apartment near the iconic Walk of Fame, alongside his brother Robert. It was a leap of faith, a fresh start in pursuit of happiness and stability.

Given that she had played a pivotal role in my upbringing and had the stature of my mother, I thought Livera deserved a farewell despite her unruly conduct and unrestrained behavior. With this thought and to collect my belongings, I returned to Livera's house for one last time (I thought this was the last time I was going to see her). As I went inside of my room to gather my belongings, I was met with a heart-wrenching revelation. All of my high- fashion items, my prized possessions, had been stolen. Diablotia Dana and the jealous foster girls, the Harlots, had stripped me of everything I held dear. The old me would have sat on the floor and cried in that moment, but spending time with Dylan had made me a new person. So I packed whatever was left in the cupboard, walked out the door, and headed straight to the waiting taxi parked outside. I was not going to allow Livera's toxicity to further ruin my mental health. I set my sights on building a new life with Dylan, free from the shadows of the past.

As the year unfolded, Dylan and I began our life together, eagerly awaiting the arrival of our first child. In 1996, our son entered the world, filling our lives with immeasurable joy and love. Later that year, we exchanged vows and officially became husband and wife, solidifying our commitment to each other and our growing family. We worked tirelessly to provide for our son, each taking on responsibilities and striving for a brighter future.

While challenges and uncertainties loomed over us, we found solace in the moments of joy and togetherness. We savored outings to restaurants, movie nights, and shopping sprees, relishing the simple pleasures that life had to offer. Santa Monica Beach became a cherished escape, a place where we could unwind and create lasting memories.

Though the path ahead was not without its hardships, we navigated the trials together, driven by our love for our son and the determination to build a stable life. Dylan worked tirelessly, taking on two jobs to provide for our family, while I secured a position at Bank of America. Money flowed in, and we reveled in the joys of parenthood, cherishing the bond we shared as husband and wife.

As the years passed, we were reminded of the difficulties that come with maintaining a relationship, especially in a city like Los Angeles, where distractions abound. Growing up in Rialto, California, I was no stranger to the challenges that awaited us. Yet, despite the trials that awaited, we clung to the memories of happiness and fulfillment, drawing strength from the love we had built.

In the year 2000, another blessing graced our lives as Willow and Dylan welcomed their second son into the world. Like his older brother, he was healthy and beautiful, a testament to the love shared between his parents. The joy of parenthood filled their hearts once more, and for a while, their happiness seemed unshakeable.

But as time wore on, Dylan and I began to face challenges that tested the strength of our relationship. Serious issues arose, and despite our best efforts, we found ourselves drifting apart. Eventually, we made the difficult decision to separate, noticing that our paths were diverging in different directions. Moving away from a cherished attachment, I was once again seeking solace and support from a friend or even a stranger that would hold me and say, "Everything will be alright." I turned to the familiar embrace of my hometown, Rialto.

It was Livera who extended a welcoming hand, offering me the opportunity to return to her fold. The matriarch's heart softened as she witnessed the struggles her adoptive daughter. She opened her doors once more, showering Willow and her boys with kindness and concern. Livera's own daughter, Diablotia bore a warm presence this time around. The mother and her daughter had moved to a spacious, two-story home that provided ample room for me and my boys.

The reunion with her extended family was nothing short of heartwarming. Relatives from near and far flocked to see me, offering advice and unwavering support. It was as if they had missed my presence ever since I had left back in '94. Livera, in particular, proved to be a pillar of support, willingly taking on the role of a doting babysitter without expecting any rent or cash in return of her services. She even insisted that I take some time off work, but I refused her advice as I was aware of my responsibilities as a mother. My job in Glendale, California, provided the means to care for my babies, and I was determined to fulfill my role to the best of my ability.

Whether it was driving or taking the Metrolink, I ensured that I was present each day and not skip a day at work. The challenges of raising kids without a father never graced my face and the customers I dealt with were extremely satisfied with the support I provided them. I cherished my employment that both sustained me and allowed me to care for my beloved sons. The routine became a source of stability amid the uncertainty of my personal life. Willow found solace in the familiarity of her job, finding fulfillment in the daily tasks that provided for her family's needs.

Chapter 7 -
Life's Unexpected Turns

As I settled into my new life as a single mother, contentment enveloped me. Raising my boys and maintaining my job at Bank of America kept me grounded and sane amidst life's challenges. Each day brought a sense of fulfillment as I balanced my responsibilities and cherished moments with my children. I would wake up half past six sharp, take a shower and then prepare dinner for my kids and myself. Livera would sometimes help around in the kitchen seeing me juggle things. Once the breakfast was ready, I would awake my boys with a kiss to their foreheads. My boys were the epitome of God's created Angels. They had naturally sensed that their mother was going through a lot, and therefore, they didn't trouble me in the slightest manner. It was either that, or the Lord had decided to give me disciplined kids in exchange for the troubles of my own childhood. My kids were respectful, obedient, and well-behaved and I was thriving in my job at the Bank of America. My life was bearable for the first time in quite a while, but little did I know that a sudden twist of fate would once again alter the course of my journey.

Out of the blue, Dylan, my ex-partner, made a surprise visit to Livera's house in Rialto. The doorbell rang, and as Livera answered it, she informed me that Dylan had come to see me. I couldn't help but wonder how he had managed to find my address. I didn't have to wonder for long because I soon realized that Dylan's older cousin's wife, who was the in-law of an in-law, must have informed him of my residence. Livera invited him in and I stood in the passageway with my arms crossed, waiting to see his face once again. He came to the hallway and smiled upon seeing me. I didn't smile back and only gazed at him with an expression less face, making desist his smile. He gave his greetings and asked how I was doing. I gave him nonchalant answers. As were conversed, I noticed that he was carrying a small suitcase with him. I inquired about it and he asked me to call the kids, saying that it contained a few things for the kids. I called my boys into the hall; they came running and were excited to see their father.

After hugging his sons tightly, Dylan told them to sit tightly and proceeded to open his suitcase. The suitcase was full of new clothes; he had brought them on his way to Rialto. He began unpacking clothes he had bought for the kids, but this unexpected gesture alone was not enough to rekindle our relationship. I appreciated his efforts, but we had grown apart over the past year, and mere gifts from Hollywood wouldn't bridge that divide. I was almost certain but not totally sure that his gestures wouldn't bridge the gap between us. You see, Dylan had this charm, this unspoken attraction that made him desirable to any woman. He could do the worst yet still make his way back into anyone's life, using his magnetism and appeal. He did the same with me then, forcing me not to refuse his offer to reconnect.

Anyways, we started talking on the phone, cautiously navigating our way through the tangled webs of our past. In 2001, after receiving my tax return, I treated myself to a new car, and I decided to drive to visit an in-law of an in- law. It was Dylan's older cousin's wife who had discreetly shared my whereabouts with him. With my shiny new car, I embarked on the journey, ready to face whatever awaited me.

I parked right outside of the in-law's house. To my surprise, Dylan's mother, Demi, was present when I joined everyone inside the house. The atmosphere was cordial, and everyone seemed genuinely happy to see me. The wife of Dylan's cousin didn't tell me that she had invited almost the entire family. I was greeting and meeting everyone in succession, but Dylan was nowhere to be seen. He then came out from the upstairs room, dressed sharply and exuding a newfound confidence. It appeared to me that my ex-mother in law and the cousin's wife had set me up for this meeting; however, I decided to go ahead with it regardless.

In our meeting, Dylan and I conversed on many topics, from my job to our kids. This whole set-up wasn't bad either, especially the food. It was good for me to finally remove myself from my hectic life and breathe a little. It had been some time since I had arrived at this meeting. I looked at my wrist watch and realized that it was getting late, so I decided to excuse myself from Dylan and his family.

Dylan requested to see me off and I accepted the request. After indulging me in a short conversation right outside at the porch of the house, Dylan expressed his apologies and pleaded for my forgiveness. Though his words had been uttered before, this time there was a rawness to his emotions. I was thinking of my response and then out of nowhere, he dropped to his knees and wrapped his arms around my legs. I felt a sudden wetness on the front of my thigh, realizing that it was his tears streaming down his face. It was a scene that left both me and his cousin's wife dumbfounded.

I gently urged Dylan to stand up, assuring him that I would take time to think about his plea. When I was inside attending their little get-together, Demi and a gathering of familiar faces were also expressing their unwavering support, sharing stories of how Dylan constantly spoke of me and our boys.

They had emphasized Dylan's desire to reunite our family, to reclaim what had been lost.

I had always held a strong belief in second chances, and this transformed version of Dylan appeared to be an entirely different person. Thus, I made the choice to extend another opportunity to him, convinced that he had gleaned wisdom from his past mistakes and firmly believing that he wouldn't shatter my heart once again.

Over time, against the backdrop of our shared history, we managed to find our way back to each other. Dylan relocated to Rialto, and we embarked on a fresh chapter of our lives together in my new apartment. The routine of commuting from Rialto to Glendale became a familiar one, with me dropping him off before heading to my own job. We had organized daycare with a trusted friend who cared for my boys while I worked, providing invaluable support during those long hours.

I earnestly desired for our relationship to succeed, primarily because our children needed the love and attention of both their parents, not just one. I prayed that the separation had imparted a valuable lesson to Dylan and that he would finally step into the role of a responsible person, and more importantly, a dedicated father.

However, as our journey together progressed, it took an unexpected turn. Dylan inexplicably quit his job, leaving me to commute to Glendale alone. The strain of the distance, coupled with his sudden unemployment, began to chip away at the stability we had sought. Our financial struggles deepened, and doubts crept into my mind. I questioned whether Dylan was bringing other women into our home while I was away, as he would invite his single friends over, something that fueled my insecurities. The fleeting thought of him bringing other women over to my house, all the whileI was draining myself far away to provide for this family, disgusted me.

The cracks in our marriage widened, and the strain became unbearable.

Our relationship teetered on the edge once again, this time due to Dylan's unexpected job changes. Dylan had managed to secure a security guard's job at someplace while I worked at Sears Credit. The job didn't require him to struggle endlessly as people weren't carrying out robberies or any other criminal activities daily. All he was required to do was to stake out suspicious individuals and activities from the comforts of security room and then receive a hefty check at the end of the month. He couldn't even manage that and decided to quit his job once again.

Our arguments increased ten folds, forming a wedge between us. It all came to a head during a heated argument as he drove us home one day. He became furious and started driving recklessly when I asked him if he had found himself a new job. Fueled by frustration, he intentionally hit a curb that caused our car to flip over twice before coming to a stop in the middle of the road.

Miraculously, I survived the accident, though shaken to my core. He sustained a few scratches but managed to escape death unscathed. As the police arrived on the scene, I expressed my suspicion that he had intentionally put our lives in danger. They detained him temporarily, but he was later released.

Following this incident, I realized that our marriage had reached its breaking point once again. It was time to make a permanent decision for the sake of our children's well-being. Dylan understood my reasons for wanting to distance myself from him, and together, we made peace. It was now crucial to focus on what was best for our boys.

Months passed, and one of Dylan's friends flagged me down, informing me that he was living across the street from our old apartments in an abandoned motel. His friends attempted to gaslight me into believing that women were sympathetic in nature and that I should forgive him and take him back. But I remained resolute, knowing deep in my heart that our relationship had run its course. I would pass by his motel on my way to work, a bittersweet reminder of what once was.

One day, Dylan's friend sent me his message, conveying that he desired to speak with me. I obliged, and we had a mature conversation. He expressed his intentions to return to Los Angeles but assured me that he cared for the kids. I was listening to what he had to say, and then he requested that I extend my hand. I was hesitant at first but then he told me to have some faith. I cautiously extended my hand towards him, and he placed a stack of banknotes on it, saying that I was a little something for me and the kids.

We parted ways, wishing each other well, never knowing that it would be our final conversation. The devastating news arrived on November 6, 2001.

Dylan had been killed by one of his friends, a person who had visited our home in the past. My world shattered, and the grief would linger for years to come.

Life had dealt me a painful blow, and I struggled to make sense of it all. He was not the perfect man by any means. To some extent, he was a child entrapped in a man's body. All he ever wanted was to have fun and not think about the future as we navigated the course of our life together. In hindsight, I believe the responsibility of raising a child had shaken him and he was unable to cope with the burden. He had made mistakes and he willing accepted that he was wrong on so many occasion. To me that is one of the many characteristics of a real man. Again, he wasn't inherently a bad man. The inequality of resources, especially during the times we were brought up in, made him act like a bad person at times.

The memories we shared were hard to forget. And so, with a heavy heart and a renewed sense of determination to do good for my kids and inspired by my once loving husband's memory, I embarked on the next chapter of my life, ready to face whatever lay ahead.

Chapter 8 –

Lionel and Lies

In 2004, I entered into a spiritual union and relocated to Houston the following year with my then-life partner, Lionel. In 2005, with the support of my spiritual partner, I welcomed another baby into the world—a boy. It seemed the girly genes weren't in my favor after all. After giving birth, my husband and I made the decision to make Houston our permanent home, partly influenced by an unforeseen emergency.

Our move to Houston brought with it some enjoyable moments as we adapted to our new surroundings. While I was earning a decent income, it wasn't sufficient to enable us to purchase a house for our growing family. With our boys getting older, it became apparent that we needed to boost our income to meet their expanding needs.

Despite my efforts to encourage my spouse to seek stable employment and improve our financial situation, he consistently fell short of his promises. Much as it pains me to admit it now, the patterns in my relationship with my then-life partner resembled those I had experienced with

Dylan. He would become agitated whenever I broached the subject of employment, and when I raised concerns during his good moods, he swiftly changed the subject, acting as if our financial struggles would magically resolve themselves.

Adding to my frustration, he continually advocated for polygamy, as his beliefs differed from mine. Furthermore, when I was away at work, he displayed an abusive nature toward my elder boys because they weren't his own, which ultimately became the catalyst for our divorce.

His abuse was hidden and started in 2009 right around the time we divorced when I really caught him and my eldest son confirmed it.

Ironically, he accused me of infidelity, despite my unwavering loyalty.

Our relationship encountered its share of challenges. I later discovered that he was staying in touch with women from his past using a calling card, which heightened my suspicions. Moreover, his persistent efforts to pressure me into accepting polygamy by converting my religion only added to my doubts about his true intentions. It was perplexing, but that man seemed to possess a high level of sexual energy. I couldn't confirm whether it was due to elevated testosterone levels, a family history of high libido men, or simply his nature.

In the midst of these uncertainties, I found myself pregnant with my second child, right around the time we were scheduled for a postpartum check-up at the hospital. Postpartum check-ups involve assessing the mother's blood pressure, weight, breasts, and abdomen after childbirth. So there I was in the hospital, accompanied by Lionel, when the medical attendant informed us that I was expecting another child. It was quite shocking initially, but I felt gratitude towards God for blessing me with another baby, especially when there were women in my vicinity who struggled with infertility.

He was consistent with his red flags but being a victim of my considerate nature, I chose to give him time in the hopes that he would change. Admittedly, things seemed promising at the start of our life in Houston from the years 2005 to 2007. However,as the year 2008 came about, it became apparent that our situation wasn't improving. Lionel did not show any inclination to change, so finally, in the year 2008, I filed for divorce. Not to mention, in 2009 it was confirmed that he had been abusive to all my boys, especially my eldest that had showed me and told me what transpired while I was at work until 9 pm.

Consequently, in the same year, five years after our marriage, I made the difficult decision to file for a divorce. Fortunately, in Houston, Texas, the process was more affordable compared to the other states in America.

The city offered applicants a waiver of service divorce, which finalized the legal proceedings within 30 days and Lionel agreed and signed off on the divorce.

As the court date for our divorce approached, my then-life partner unexpectedly began contesting the divorce, introducing further complications into the process.

After the conclusion of this life-altering journey was eventually finalized, my former significant other started harassing me and made false reports to Child Protective Services (CPS), leading me to seek legal assistance to refute these baseless claims. Thanks to my outstanding attorney, all the fabricated reports were dismissed, and we were able to secure a lifelong protection order for both me and my sons. Once again, I witnessed God's mercy in my life, as my attorney astutely added a clause to my divorce agreement that I had overlooked.

My attorney, whom I am truly grateful for, successfully negotiated child support into our arrangement, which had been absent from the initial agreement. This inclusion was crucial and would significantly impact my situation. While the modest amount of two hundred and fifty dollars a month wouldn't make or break me, it was a fair contribution based on what I believed my husband's income to be. Despite being financially stable and fully capable of raising my boys on my own without a cent from him, it was disheartening that he chose not to attend the final hearing of our divorce proceedings to disclose his true financial worth. Spoiler alert: My husband was wealthy, and I had been unaware of it.

Once again, God was in my corner telling my attorney that she needed to transcribe child support on the divorce file.

Life began to look brighter once again as my sons and I moved forward, and I met someone new in 2009. We decided to take things slow and developed a friendship that turned into a long-lasting love that has a strong foundation of loyalty and true commitment. The two of us are engaged to be married in the near future. My new good man was a breath of fresh air and helped me get through my divorce and court process while being a calming force for me because I was in shock and ready to retaliate - real talk! He was so fine to me and ambitious, holding down a career when I met him for 10 years. I was really impressed with his go-getter persona and his dedication to his daughter. He loved my boys and would provide gifts, money, and support for all of us as I kept going to court appearance after court appearance, fighting possible charges and trying to finalize our already agreed-to divorce.

While life seemed to look great once again, unfortunately, it took an unexpected turn when my children started facing problems at their school, experiencing harassment and bullying.

I had the utmost trust in my boys. From their childhood, they were intrigued by everything and anything that stroked their curiosity. When I took them to outings like Chuck E Cheese, to the movies, bowling, church, skating, and fine dining, I remember them always being mature and happy, bonding as brothers do, and having the time of their lives. So, being their mother and raising them well, I knew that they hadn't invited the bullying or harassment by getting into fights or being aggressive first!

When they shared their troubles with me, it became evident that these issues were somehow connected to my ex-life partner.

Determined to get to the bottom of it, I started investigating the matter.

I made frequent visits to the Alief manager's office to understand the connection between the bullying and the physical abuse. During one of these visits, the manager informed me that he wanted to ensure the lifetime protection order was recognized and included in my divorce arrangement and wanted to update his data bases. The manager also required my ex-husband's updated address for their records. Given that my ex-husband and I no longer communicated, I turned to Google to find his new address. My intention was to simply find his address and then dictate it to the Alief manager, however, with that Google search, I stumbled upon something surprising he had been hiding from me.

It turned out that he had won a lottery in the year 2016 in a different state during the time I was filing for divorce. This revelation was shocking because one of the reasons for our separation was his unwillingness to find stable work andcontribute to our family's financial responsibilities. He had portrayed himself as someone uninterested in improving our lifestyle and supporting our kids' needs, yet he was sitting on a substantial amount of money from the lottery win. As I pondered this revelation, it only added another layer of complexity to our past issues and raised further questions about his true intentions during our marriage.

Gradually, the pieces of the puzzle began to fit together as I discerned the recurring patterns: the enigmatic phone calls to other women via a calling card, his persistent avoidance of employment and job interviews, and the clever ruse he employed to hide his lottery win. It suddenly became clear that he had actually won the lottery while our divorce proceedings were underway. His deceit was astonishing; he intentionally presented himself as financially destitute during the court hearings, all the while secretly amassing millions of dollars. His cunning strategy aimed to downplay the value of his winnings, knowing that they would have been subject to division had they come to light earlier in our divorce proceedings.

If I had known about his financial windfall, I would have certainly asked for my share ensured my children received their fair portion during the divorce proceedings.

As for the troubles at my boys' school, the harassment and bullying they faced could be linked to possible retaliation from my ex-husband's family, as I had emerged victorious in court, defeating their precious son, brother, or relative. I promptly informed both the school and the police about the ongoing issues, but unfortunately, the problems persisted from 2010 through 2023, coinciding with my efforts to recover my remains of my embezzled trust.

Adding to my already challenging situation, certain members of my second husband's extended family relocated to Houston secretly. These individuals, somehow related to him, began conspiring against me and my children. Not to mention the foster frauds and a few of my former classmates were secretly made aware of my circumstances and decide to get involved in my sufferings. Their actions escalated into a disturbing series of stalking, job fraud, identity theft, assault, harassment and vandalism.

I was constantly in the state of lookout; inspecting every passing stranger, staring at every suspicious parked vehicle, answering my door with holding a stern object behind my back, and stayingan additional few minutes outside my boys' school to ensure they reach their class without any complications.

The family of my ex lifetime partner, Lionel was resolute in showing his ugly side due to the disgust they had for my precious family.As time went on, their threats escalated to dangerous levels, and they resorted to extreme actions. Shockingly, they even involved their relatives whom I had never met or known to reside in Houston.

In a horrifying incident, a disturbed member of their family attempted to shoot my middle son multiple times. I was also struck by a stray bullet during that terrifying episode, though fortunately, I was only grazed.

Then, on February 14, 2023, a boy from Lionel's family, who had been feigning friendship with my middle son, arrived at my front door and attempted to shoot my son to death. Thankfully, his aim was poor, but my son still suffered a gunshot wounds, and the subsequent events are too painful to discuss.

With that being said, the gravity of this situation cannot be understated, as he could have easily harmed my sons or myself if I had been home at that moment.

The events I have shared in this chapter are just a few of the many harrowing accounts of the dangers my family and I faced, enduring threats, violence, and relentless harassment from Dylan's and my second husband's spiteful families and their wives.

Throughout all the challenges and hardships these life events have given me, I've come to realize that there's a direct connection betweenthe difficulties I've encountered and my spiritual journey and purpose in life. Life's setbacks and struggles have tested my faith, pushing me to seek solutions on my own. Despite the chaos that unfolded for years, I never stopped praying for my boys and their well-being. My biggest priority was to protect them and guide them away from the wrong paths, avoiding the allure of the street life, and the dangers and traps setup by the obvious.

Amid financial setbacks in some capacity, I fervently prayed for a better career and relief from oppression. My most heartfelt plea was for God's protection against any harm, hurt, or danger that might come our way.

Now that all my boys have grown into adulthood, I am fully devoted to being a guiding presence in their lives and making sure they walk the path of virtue. My youngest son, along with his brothers, is destined for greatness, and I am determined to nurture them with unwavering love and dedication

Despite the setbacks, oppression, violence, and stalking that we faced,I consistently sought help and support from my family, school personnel, and the Police to maintain order and protect my family and my life-time protection order. As a single mother, raising my boys has been like having another full-time job, but it's also been an incredibly rewarding one.

The unconditional love I have for my children and their love for me as their mother, serves as a driving force to keep pushing forward and striving for a better future for all of us.

Chapter 9 -

A Journey to Self- Discovery and Empowerment

As each day passed, I found myself embodying the stereotype of the "Woman in her forties." My life had been a journey through various trials and tribulations. I was separated from my mother at a tender age and subjected to harsh living conditions. Thankfully, I was fortunate to find my first loving and compassionate adoptive family, a true home where family values prevailed.

Conversely, my experience with the second family that sought to adopt me was starkly different. They were cold-hearted and displayed no empathy. In fact, the court even hesitated to grant them legal guardianship over me. Unfortunately, I had to endure living in two contrasting foster care environments until, at long last, one of them was officially approved to adopt me.

I had fallen in love, then again, and then finally fallen in disgust of a person that I once loved. My life had been a whirlwind of experiences, a rollercoaster ride of triumphs and tribulations. From the joy of bringing my wonderful boys into the world to enduring the pain of multiple divorces, assault, stalking, and identity theft, I had faced challenges that pushed me to my limits. Through it all, one constant emerged – some of my former in-laws, a group determined to make my life a living hell.

The previous chapter covers most of the happenings where some of Dylan's and some of my second husband's family showed their ugly side. Just to give more context about our victimization through their relentless bullying, they didn't stop with their harassment even when I pressed charges for the attempted murder of my son. This aligns with the gravity of the second shooting. I can't speak about it because my tears won't cease, and my heart remains broken. I am still in complete shock. During the time when the kids and I were inside our home, my instincts ensured that our front gate was locked. In the nights especially, my small family was terrified of going outside because our oppressors could be lurking in the dark, waiting for us to make a wrong move.

The relentless harassment knew no bounds, and this craziness involved some of their mistresses, corruption, and even some of my former friends from my childhood who were secretly jealous of me and seemed to desire my life.

They seemed to revel in conspiring against me and my children, stalking our every move, and subjecting us to acts of vandalism. It was as if they were on a mission to break my spirit, to make me look mentally incapacitated, and to see me crumble under the weight of their malevolence.

The constant harassment and the uncalled for aggression had changed me. Before all of this, I would look in the mirror and see myself as a personification of a butterfly – soft and charming, with genuine thoughtfulness for everyone. However, with everything going on, my thoughts were plagued and my mind had travelled to darker places. I knew the people who were intending harm to my kids. I had seen their faces and even dined in with some. I had faith in the police, but at the same time, I was aware that they had to follow a procedure before they could make any arrests. So naturally, my biggest concern was, "What is this about?"

Is it because I moved on with my life, or is it about control and greed? Back then, I was unaware that money or a real barrier of obsession and control were part of their agendas!

No mother would relegate the safety of her child to a department that already has thousands of criminal cases on their hands because she loves her child more than the department would care for. She would do the necessary, even if it requires me to take a stand and send a real direct message to them all about mine. I couldn't break the law because who would be there for my babies? Who could even come close to the mother's love that I have for my kids? A love that could never be matched. As life would have it, I found myself in a disadvantaged situation, and my thoughts, which were once bright and lively, had turned darker.

I never thought I would resort to self-defense methods, and now I find myself in a situation where my family's connections with influential people might come to my aid, something I never anticipated. The person I used to be couldn't fathom dealing with this. I could never comprehend why someone would need a gun for protection, especially when living in a nice area and abiding by the law.

In addition to harboring negative thoughts about people who carried firearms, the very individuals who bore arms ignited anger and confusion within me. Firearms instilled terror in the hearts of observers. Regrettably, the behavior of my extended family in the past had tested my patience severely, and I felt a strong urge to take decisive action.

After my son and I were shot at in 2020, I began conducting thorough research on gun ownership, and I had the necessary funds to buy one for myself. I was thinking logically, trying to suppress my emotional side. The safety of your children comes first.

There are laws for self-defense, particularly stand your ground laws. So, I did it the right way and obtained the proper clearances and registrations, making that purchase back in 2022. I knew that God was my protector and that he can strike someone down, and he walks with me, he talks with me, and he reassures me that he is God all by himself!

To this day, I have not had to fire, pull out, or mention that I have a gun. I further realized that the struggle I was going through was nothing but a trial from God, bestowed on my shoulders to make me stronger.

But, as life's trials often do, these challenges unintentionally brought me closer to spirituality. In the midst of chaos, I turned to God for support and guidance. Of course, my foremost prayers were directed at the safety of my family, but as I witnessed God's protection in action, I began to seek His blessings for my personal growth and career.

My journey towards self-discovery and empowerment began with a shift in mindset. I realized that despite my numerous qualifications, the opportunities that came my way did not match my potential and education. I had always been ambitious and determined to create the best life for myself and my family. With each setback, I grew more determined to find success on my own terms.

I had entrusted the responsibility of looking after my kids to God, and I had unwavering faith in His care for them. With the assurance that my kids were well taken care of, I delved into the realm of academia, exploring subjects and degrees that would enhance my skills and knowledge. I had to be extra careful while selecting the certificates to pursue and the degrees to register for because the skills I would acquire from them would make me an attractive prospect in the white- collar job market. For the most of my life, the idea of learning about new things fascinated me, and therefore, my thirst for knowledge led me to pursue a technical writing certificate from the University of Houston in 2015. With this new skillset, I decided to step away from performing X- rays, where I held a certificate as a Licensed Medical Radiologic Technologist (LMRT) since 2007 I knew it was time toexplore new horizons.

In 2017, I accomplished another milestone by earning a bachelor's degree in General Studies/Communication. This educational pursuit opened my eyes to the power of effective communication and equipped me with essential skills for the corporate world.

In 2018, I also obtained my state license in Life and Health Insurance, and as of today, I hold licenses in numerous states.

But my quest for knowledge didn't stop there. Fueled by a desire to broaden my expertise and deepen my understanding of business, I embarked on a journey to pursue a Master's Degree in Business Management. In 2020, I proudly graduated with a Master's Degree, armed with knowledge that had the potential to reshape the course of my life.

With this newfound education and experience, I yearned to carve out my own path, aiming to become a business owner and employ my degree in a management role within the corporate sector. I recognized the necessity of shifting my mindset and perspective to fully embrace the world of business, aligning it with my future goals and objectives. This transition from an employee mindset to a business owner's mindset demanded a fundamental paradigm shift, one that required unwavering determination, creativity, and resilience.

Education became my guiding light, leading me through uncharted territory. I delved into the intricacies of the business world, understanding the importance of networking, marketing, and branding. Empowered by knowledge and determination, I ventured into the realm of entrepreneurship with a clear vision of my aspirations.

As I delved deeper into the world of business, I came to realize the paramount importance of adopting a business mindset. It marked a complete departure from working for someone else to taking the helm of my own ship.

My knowledge continued to expand, and I grew wiser with each passing day. I distinctly remember one of the early instances where I applied my academic knowledge to the real world — when I began developing my brands. Utilizing my insurance license, I raised a portion of the capital needed for my businesses. This approach proved to be a valuable means of mitigating risks as I worked to get my businesses off the ground.

I embraced the challenges and the uncertainty, knowing that every obstacle was an opportunity for growth. The part of my life that was solely granted to education still seams unreal. The reason why I completed the bachelor's degree in General Studies and Communication was so I could become a valuable asset in the local white-collar job market. I had been content with doing a regular job that tested my skills and paid a hefty check in the end, covering all my expenses and my boys' school fees. However, God had other plans, and indeed, they were better than mine.

"Man plans and then God plans, and indeed God's plan willalways be better."

My education and personal growth also instilled in me the importance of self-belief. I no longer settled for mediocrity or limited myself by self-doubt. Instead, I acknowledged my worth and sought opportunities that aligned with my passion and potential.

While the journey was not without its hurdles, my education and newfound mindset propelled me forward. I learned to navigate the complexities of entrepreneurship, making strategic decisions that aligned with my vision. I once believed that my identity was that of an ordinary woman, one who wakes up every day, sends her kids to school, and then goes to her place of employment, returning home around 6 or 7 pm. To tell the truth, I would have been extremely content with that lifestyle because any woman who works and takes care of her children deserves great admiration, perhaps a little more than men.

However, I like to believe that it was God's plan all along to use me as a vessel for His blessings in exchange for the trials and tribulations I've endured. The Lord intended for me to inspire young women facing similar challenges. I've read that everything in life is interconnected, and now, being in a place I could only dream of as a child, I wholeheartedly agree with that notion. The wisdom and triumphs conveyed in Holy Books may not always resonate with us humans because, in the end, they are stories. We tend to relate more to tangible examples, which might be why God chose to make me a living, breathing illustration of what life can become through hard work and righteous intentions.

He decided to use me as a conduit for His message, and now I am chronicling my journey in this book so that the next young woman who picks it up knows that she is not alone in her struggles and that God is always by her side, helping her realize the dreams she held since childhood.

After tapping into my potential, I ventured into entrepreneurship, and my professional career brimmed with fresh opportunities. Over time, I had access to numerous online business prospects. My previous sense of helplessness has now evolved, and I have become an inspirational figure for women who have encountered various challenges.

I am still expanding my businesses and emphasizing how mindset and academic achievements are interconnected with reaching one's full potential, especially when it comes to building one's brand and positioning for business ownership. My success thus far lies in being an independent insurance agent, while my online platforms are still in the development and refinement stage.

In 2016, I enrolled in the Teacher Certification Program and have diligently worked towards becoming a certified teacher ever since. Currently, I am focused on studying additional material to prepare for this career. Simultaneously, I am pursuing a second Masters Degree in online teaching to ensure I am well-prepared for my future endeavors.

Having a business-oriented mindset, I comprehend the importance of diversifying income streams. The thriving landscape of online ecommerce businesses offers an excellent opportunity for me to pursue two careers and witness the growth of my online platforms, contributing to my overall financial stability. Given the uncertainties of the economy, it's essential to have contingency plans like Plan B, C, and D.

Incorporating these career paths into my life not only fulfills my passion for teaching but also provides financial security and the ability to adapt to changing circumstances. It's empowering to know that I am diversifying my skills and resources, setting myself up for a future of continued growth and success.

As I embarked on this new chapter, I understood that success was not just about financial gain but about creating a fulfilling life for myself and my children. My education had unlocked the doors to new possibilities, and I was determined to make the most of it.

Life's challenges had shown me the strength within me, and my spirituality had provided solace and guidance. I was no longer confined by the shackles of my past; instead, I soared with the wings of knowledge and empowerment.

Through education and a changed mindset, I evolved into an accomplished woman, ready to take on the world. I looked forward to the future with a sense of excitement and purpose, knowing that with determination and faith, there was no limit to what I could achieve. My journey of self-discovery and empowerment had just begun, and I was ready to embrace every opportunity that came my way.

Chapter 10 -
Unveiling the Path to Success: Lessons from Adversity

Life's journey is a tapestry of challenges and triumphs, a mosaic of setbacks and successes. Through the twists and turns of my own tumultuous path, I've discovered the secrets to harnessing the power of a business mindset and building multiple streams of income. I've walked through the fire of adversity and emerged stronger, wiser, and determined to share the lessons I've learned with others who are on a similar quest for success.

The episode of bullying of my boys had ended and we were finally looking forward to welcome contentment in our lives. This time, there were no twists and turns; sunlight was gleaming directly inside our house, and there were no casting shadows. It was a way of God telling us that "everything will be, or was, alright." And surely, I wasn't doubting God at that moment because it certainly felt different: the gleaming light, the warm yet cozy temperature, and the unheard sound of serenity with birds chirping. The singing of birds, in particular, made me feel content because I had read somewhere that birds sing in places where they don't sense any fear. Observing all that calmness in my surroundings, I could only think that God had blessed us.

This entire book has documented my life as a young girl, then as a teenager, and finally as an adult and the mother of all my bright young boys. The one constant of my journey has been grappling with struggles. Now, as this book reaches its conclusion, I want to offer something to you for bearing with me and reading my story with dedication. I wish to give you suggestion and some practical advice on how to pass through your dealings with struggle. I sincerely hope that you emerge as a better person and, more importantly, achieve victory over whatever you are struggling with. If you are struggling to make ends meet as an entrepreneur, I hope that my journey as an entrepreneur will inspire you, and my practical advice will offer support in realizing your entrepreneurial dreams.

When you're in the throes of struggle, it's essential to reframe your thoughts and shield yourself from negativity. Surround yourself with those who uplift and inspire, and keep your distance from dream snatchers and naysayers. Your focus should remain unyielding, fixated on your goals, achievements, and aspirations. Remember, you are the architect of your destiny, capable of shaping your reality through sheer determination and perseverance.

Before deciding on becoming an entrepreneur, you must have thought to yourself that business owner make more money than employees. You may have come to the conclusion that being a business owner is more rewarding, albeit with greater risks attached. Consequently, you chose to leave your steady job and become a business owner, similar to many business tycoons in America today.

If you weren't already aware, one of the most common questions posed by aspiring entrepreneurs is the same one you asked yourself before deciding to become an entrepreneur for the rest of your life. The question is whether employees or business owners make more money. The answer, while nuanced, lies in the potential of business ownership. Unlike employees confined to a fixed salary, business owners have the capacity to unlock unlimited earning potential. However, the magnitude of a business owner's income hinges on the prosperity of their enterprise. Industry, business size, and employee experience are all contributing factors that influence this dynamic.

Yet, the merits of being a business owner extend beyond financial gain. Business owners possess a competitive edge, fueled by their expertise, talents, and innovative business models. This expertise not only drives revenue but also enhances overall profitability, leading to a higher income potential compared to traditional employment.

While it is true that you may be struggling as an entrepreneur; there is no shaming in admitting that. You may even struggle for longer than you anticipated, but here's the catch, your struggles won't last forever. Perhaps tomorrow, next month, or even a year later, I am certain that your struggles will come to an end. I am certain because I am speaking from experience. I, too, initially struggled with my online businesses and as an entrepreneur, but all of my worries were eventually resolved because I remained focused on my goals, true to my work ethics, and held good intentions with my businesses.

You could say that I am validating you when I say that you made the right choice of quitting your job and becoming an entrepreneur. There is nothing wrong in being an employee at an organization but the benefits of being an owner are incomparable. As an employee or a staff member, you commit to completing specific responsibilities in exchange for a predetermined payment rate. You receive regular compensation, whether weekly, bi-weekly, or monthly, which arrives after taxes, deductions, and benefits have been subtracted. The added benefits of employment at a prestigious organization could be salary increases, access to a company vehicle, club memberships, paid time off, and healthcare packages to immediate and extended family.

Other than the stated and contractual perks, if you are an employee, your income will remain constant regardless of the company's performance.

This is a relief, especially considering that the entire world was on lockdown for months, and employees were being paid monthly by their employers to take care of their expenses. Concerns about the company's financial well-being do not affect employees, who enjoy a steady income and benefits as long as they fulfill their job obligations.

However, employees do not have a guaranteed share in the company's financial success. There is a limit to how much they can earn even if the company prospers. Employees lack control over their pay and the timing of raises. Their advancement and professional growth opportunities might be restricted, potentially confining them to their initial job role.

On the hand, individuals who own businesses might experience irregular earnings. Entrepreneurs like yourselfalso fall under this category because they eventually become business owners one day. As an entrepreneur and then eventually as an owner of small to medium sized business, the profitability your business will be uncertain because of its newly established nature. At that stage, you should be grateful instead of being stressed or disappointed. Remember not all entrepreneurs transform into business owners easily. You should ideally be motivated and invigorated at that stage because you have an entire business in front of you that needs your energy and highest attention. If you are nearing the start of your business, remember not to dwell too much on your salary, as determining an appropriate owner's salary can be a contentious issue for small business proprietors.

Determining an owner's salary isn't a one-size-fits-all approach. It hinges on variables like business type, ownership structure, operational expenditures, and other factors. Nonetheless, every business owner should allocate a payment to themselves.

During the initial stages of your business, you might be the sole employee and thus able to draw a substantial salary. However, with expansion, you'll need to recruit other personnel and cover their remunerations, potentially leading to a reduction in your own pay as they assist in lightening your workload.

Ultimately, your compensation will strikes up a balance. The amount you allot yourself should reflect fair remuneration for your hard work and business concepts, yet remain reasonable enough to avoid damage to the financial structure of the company. The salary can also be influenced by your business's performance. As a business owner, you wield authority over your compensation.

As I mentioned earlier, being a business owner will always be better than being employed at someone else's company. The foundation of this declaration ultimately boils down to the disparity in income between a salaried person and the owner. I said that the amount you draw from your company should reflect the value you contribute, i.e., your work and business idea. However, I didn't imply that there is a limit to what you can draw from your company.

For business owners and prospective business owners that are entrepreneurs, there's no upper limit to their potential earnings! You can augment your income by fostering business growth, tapping into new customer bases, or venturing into fresh markets. You retain the flexibility to introduce novel products or services and adjust your pricing. You can also capitalize on tax advantages such as deductions for business outlays and investments.

The Entrepreneurial sprit and single mom-dom!

Thinking back on my journey, I see a lot of similarities with the stories of many folks who are trying to make it out there. Just like single moms who face all sorts of curveballs but still manage to rise, I've had my share of ups and downs. Life can throw you some wild twists, but if you keep your head up, you can come out on top. I've come to believe that my success isn't all just me – it's also thanks to a little divine help from above.

Calvin Coolidge had a nugget of wisdom that sticks with me: "Nothing in the world can take the place of Persistence." That means pushing through when things get tough is key. There are lots of talented folks who don't make it big because they didn't stick with it. It's a good reminder that never giving up is what paves the way to success.

One day, I was reading Isaiah 54:1-17 and it felt like God was talking straight to me. It was like a lightbulb moment, showing me that my struggles weren't in vain and that better days were ahead. It was like a pep talk from the big guy upstairs, showing me the way to my true calling.

With this new perspective, I'm stepping into a fresh

chapter of my life. I'm gunning for success and I'm not backing down. I am looking forward to completing my teaching degree with flying colors and I am excited about the path that lay in front of me. I would love to teach the new generation the miracles of life. If all my planned endeavors come to fruition and with the support of God, I aspire to establish more businesses. This time of physical nature!

For the time being, I'm aiming for a path full of chances and opportunities, not just for me but also to help others rise up. Every move I make is with purpose, like a trail of breadcrumbs leading to this point.

Getting to the top isn't a walk in the park, but I've got the right mindset, the strength to push through, and a strong sense of what I'm here for. Just like how my life took a turn for the better, I'm all about sharing the secrets of my journey. Remember, you've got greatness inside you, and with some grit and faith, you can steer your life towards amazing things. Your destiny is calling – all you need is the will to keep going, no matter what.